WORLD CUP '98

COOL KEEPERS

Written by Mark Hillsdon

The publisher would like to thank the following for their kind permission to reproduce their photographs:

a=above; b=below; c=centre; l=left; r=right; t=top.

ACTION-PLUS: 25ca; Glyn Kirk 13tc.

ACTION-PLUS/FLASH PRESS: 28bc.

ALLSPORT: Shaun Botterill 3tc, 7c; Clive Brunskill 8lc; Ben Radford 11c, 20c; Stu Forester 23tc; Mark Thompson 9c.

COLORSPORT: *Taffarel* sidebar; 4tc, 5c, 6tc, 10tc, 12bc, 15tc, 16ca, 21bc.

EMPICS: Matthew Ashton 19bc, 22c, 31c; Laurence Griffiths 18ca; Tony Marshall 24ca; Aubrey Washington 17br.

FRONT COVER
ALLSPORT: Shaun Botterill bl;
COLORSPORT: c; **EMPICS:** Laurence Griffiths cra.

PICTURE RESEARCHER: Catherine Costelloe.

FRANCE

WELCOME TO THE WORLD CUP!

France 1998 is quite simply the biggest World Cup ever! The World Cup is held every four years and this time more than 100 countries, from every corner of the globe, entered the qualifying tournament. Now 32 teams are left to compete in the finals between June 14 and July 12 1998. That's 64 matches in total, compared with just 18 at the first World Cup in Uruguay, held as long ago as 1930!

As well as being the largest tournament ever, France 1998 is only the third time that the same country has staged the finals more than once. France were also hosts in 1938; Italy and Mexico have also held the championships twice.

A player's international experience is based on the following code:

0–15 CAPS ★
16–30 CAPS ★ ★
31–45 CAPS ★ ★ ★
46–60 CAPS ★ ★ ★ ★
61+ CAPS ★ ★ ★ ★ ★

FRANCE

NAME: Fabien Barthez

BORN: 28.6.71, Lavelanet, France

HEIGHT: 6 ft (1 m 83)

CLUB SIDE: Monaco (France)

EXPERIENCE: ★

KEY FACT: Prone to errors.

AMAZING FACT: Helped Marseille win the European Champions Cup in 1993.

NAME: Bernard Lama

BORN: 7.4.63, Saint-Symphorien, France

HEIGHT: 6 ft (1 m 83)

CLUB SIDE: Paris St Germain (France)

EXPERIENCE: ★ ★ ★

KEY FACT: Superb shot stopper.

AMAZING FACT: Has appeared as a model on Parisian catwalks.

WORLD CUP 1998

3 COOL KEEPERS

BRAZIL

NAME: Cláudio André Taffarel

BORN: 5.8.66, Santa Rosa, Brazil

HEIGHT: 5 ft 11 (1 m 80)

CLUB SIDE: Athletico Mineiro (Brazil)

EXPERIENCE: ★ ★ ★ ★ ★

KEY FACT: Mr Reliable – used to the big occasion.

AMAZING FACT: Whilst unemployed in Italy during 1993, he played centre forward for the local church team.

NAME: 'Carlos Germano' Schwamback Neto

BORN: 14.8.70, Domingos Martins, Brazil

HEIGHT: 6 ft 3 (1 m 91)

CLUB SIDE: Vasco de Gama (Brazil)

EXPERIENCE: ★ ★

KEY FACT: Dependable.

NAME: David Seaman
BORN: 19.9.63, Rotherham, England
HEIGHT: 6 ft 4 (1 m 93)
CLUB SIDE: Arsenal (England)
EXPERIENCE: ★ ★ ★
KEY FACT: Penalty saving expert.
AMAZING FACT: A strong candidate for the title 'Best Goalkeeper in the World'.

NAME: Tim Flowers
BORN: 3.2.67, Kenilworth, England
HEIGHT: 6 ft 3 (1 m 91)
CLUB SIDE: Blackburn Rovers (England)
EXPERIENCE: ★
KEY FACT: Brilliant on his day but can make blunders.
AMAZING FACT: The £2.4m Blackburn paid Southampton for Flowers in November 1993 was a then British record for a goalkeeper.

WORLD CUP 1998

5 COOL KEEPERS

DENMARK

NAME: Peter Schmeichel

BORN: 18.11.63, Gladsaxe, Denmark

HEIGHT: 6 ft 3 (1 m 91)

CLUB SIDE: Manchester United (England)

EXPERIENCE: ★ ★ ★ ★ ★

KEY FACT: Superb shot-stopper and distributor of the ball.

NAME: Mogens Krogh

BORN: 31.10.63, Teers-Ugilt, Denmark

HEIGHT: 6 ft 3 (1 m 91)

CLUB SIDE: Bronby (Denmark)

EXPERIENCE: ★

KEY FACT: Great reactions and penalty expert.

AMAZING FACT: Scored for Bronby against Aarhus to win the Danish championship!

ITALY

NAME: Angelo Peruzzi

BORN: 16.2.70, Viterbo, Italy

HEIGHT: 5 ft 11 (1 m 80)

CLUB SIDE: Juventus (Italy)

EXPERIENCE: ★ ★

KEY FACT: Extremely agile.

NAME: Gianluca Pagliuca

BORN: 18.12.66, Bologna, Italy

HEIGHT: 6 ft 3 (1 m 91)

CLUB SIDE: Inter Milan (Italy)

EXPERIENCE: ★ ★ ★

KEY FACT: Thrives on one-to-one situations.

NORWAY

NAME: Frode Grodås
BORN: 24.10.64, Sogndal, Norway
HEIGHT: 6 ft 2 (1 m 88)
CLUB SIDE: Chelsea (England)
EXPERIENCE: ★ ★ ★
KEY FACT: Can drop the odd clanger.

NAME: Thomas Giil
BORN: 16.5.65, Grimstad, Norway
HEIGHT: 6 ft 2 (1 m 88)
CLUB SIDE: Duisburg (Germany)
EXPERIENCE: ★
KEY FACT: Very quick reactions.

AUSTRIA

NAME: Michael Konsel

BORN: 6.3.62, Vienna, Austria

HEIGHT: 6 ft (1 m 83)

CLUB SIDE: Roma (Italy)

EXPERIENCE: ★ ★ ★

KEY FACT: Rated as one of the best all-round keepers in the world.

NAME: Franz Wohlfahrt

BORN: 1.7.64, Sankt Veit an der Glan, Austria

HEIGHT: 6 ft 3 (1 m 91)

CLUB SIDE: Stuttgart (Germany)

EXPERIENCE: ★ ★ ★

KEY FACT: Reliable shot-stopper.

AMAZING FACT: Made the headlines in 1989 when he was hit by an iron bar thrown by a spectator during a UEFA cup game between Austria Vienna and Ajax.

BULGARIA

NAME: Boris Mikhailov

BORN: 13.2.62, Sofia, Bulgaria

HEIGHT: 6 ft 1 (1 m 85)

CLUB SIDE: Slavia Sofia (Bulgaria)

EXPERIENCE: ★ ★ ★ ★ ★

KEY FACT: A great record when it comes to saving penalties.

AMAZING FACT: He wears a wig.

NAME: Zdravko Zdravkov

BORN: 4.10.70, Sofia, Bulgaria

HEIGHT: 6 ft 1 (1 m 85)

CLUB SIDE: Buraspor (Turkey)

EXPERIENCE: ★

KEY FACT: Growing in confidence with every game.

SPAIN

NAME: Andoni Zubizarreta

BORN: 23.10.61, Vitoria, Spain

HEIGHT: 6 ft 2 (1 m 88)

CLUB SIDE: Valencia (Spain)

EXPERIENCE: ★ ★ ★ ★ ★

KEY FACT: Very experienced and used to the big occasion.

AMAZING FACT: First Spaniard to play in 100 internationals.

NAME: Ruiz Cañizares

BORN: 18.12.69, Madrid, Spain

HEIGHT: 5 ft 11 (1 m 80)

CLUB SIDE: Real Madrid (Spain)

EXPERIENCE: ★ ★

KEY FACT: Solid and imposing keeper.

BELGIUM

NAME: Gilbert Bodart

BORN: 10.9.62, Ougrée, Belgium

HEIGHT: 6 ft (1 m 83)

CLUB SIDE: Standard Liege (Belgium)

EXPERIENCE: ★ ★

KEY FACT: Quick to distribute the ball.

NAME: Filip De Wilde

BORN: 5.7.64, Zele, Belgium

HEIGHT: 5 ft 11 (1 m 80)

CLUB SIDE: Sporting Lisbon (Portugal)

EXPERIENCE: ★ ★

KEY FACT: Strong and agile.

AMAZING FACT: Took part in Italia '90 and USA '94.

HOLLAND

NAME: Edwin van der Sar

BORN: 29.10.70, Gouda, Holland

HEIGHT: 6 ft 5 (1 m 96)

CLUB SIDE: Ajax (Holland)

EXPERIENCE: ★ ★

KEY FACT: Prone to lapses in concentration.

NAME: Ed de Goey

BORN: 21.12.66, Gouda, Holland

HEIGHT: 6 ft 6 (1 m 99)

CLUB SIDE: Chelsea (England)

EXPERIENCE: ★ ★ ★

KEY FACT: His size makes him hard to beat.

AMAZING FACT: Became the most expensive goalkeeper in the Premiership when he moved from Feyenoord to Chelsea in June 1997.

YUGOSLAVIA

NAME: Ivica Kralj

BORN: 26.3.73, Tivat, Montenegro

HEIGHT: 6 ft 3 (1 m 91)

CLUB SIDE: Partisan Belgrade (Yugoslavia)

EXPERIENCE: ★ ★

KEY FACT: Moves very quickly for such a big man.

NAME: Aleksander Kocic

BORN: 18.3.69, Novi Sad, Serbia

HEIGHT: 6 ft 3 (1 m 91)

CLUB SIDE: Emploi (Italy)

EXPERIENCE: ★ ★

KEY FACT: 100% concentration throughout the game.

ROMANIA

NAME: Florin Prunea

BORN: 8.8.68, Bucharest, Romania

HEIGHT: 6 ft (1 m 83)

CLUB SIDE: Dinamo Bucharest (Romania)

EXPERIENCE: ★ ★ ★

KEY FACT: Good positional sense but weak in the air.

NAME: Bogdan Stelea

BORN: 5.12.67, Bucharest, Romania

HEIGHT: 6 ft 2 (1 m 88)

CLUB SIDE: Salamanca (Spain)

EXPERIENCE: ★ ★ ★ ★

KEY FACT: Commands his area well and is excellent in a one-to-one situation.

AMAZING FACT: A series of gaffs during USA '94 made him the target of media attacks.

GERMANY

NAME: Andreas Köpke

BORN: 12.3.62, Kiel, Germany

HEIGHT: 6 ft (1 m 83)

CLUB SIDE: Marseille (France)

EXPERIENCE: ★ ★ ★ ★

KEY FACT: All-round brilliance.

AMAZING FACT: Voted best goalkeeper in the world in 1996.

GERMANY

NAME: Oliver Kahn

BORN: 15.6.69, Karlsruhe, Germany

HEIGHT: 6 ft 2 (1 m 88)

CLUB SIDE: Bayern Munich (Germany)

EXPERIENCE: ★

KEY FACT: Excellent at collecting crosses.

AMAZING FACT: The £1.9m paid by Bayern to Karlsruhe is a record for a German goalkeeper.

CROATIA

NAME:
Drazen Ladic

BORN: 1.1.63,
Čakovec, Croatia

HEIGHT:
6 ft 1 (1 m 85)

CLUB SIDE:
Croatia Zagreb
(Croatia)

EXPERIENCE:
★ ★ ★ ★

KEY FACT:
A great record of
saving penalties.

CROATIA

NAME: Marijan Mrmic

BORN: 6.5.65, Sisak, Croatia

HEIGHT: 5 ft 11 (1 m 80)

CLUB SIDE: Besiktas (Turkey)

EXPERIENCE: ★

KEY FACT: A quiet man whose saves do the talking.

AMAZING FACT: He also works as a fireman!

SCOTLAND

NAME: Andy Goram

BORN: 13.4.64, Bury, England

HEIGHT: 5 ft 11 (1 m 80)

CLUB SIDE: Glasgow Rangers (Scotland)

EXPERIENCE: ★ ★ ★ ★

KEY FACT: Superb in one-to-one situations.

AMAZING FACT: Used to keep wicket for the Scottish cricket team!

NAME: Jim Leighton

BORN: 24.7.58, Johnstone, Scotland

HEIGHT: 6 ft 1 (1 m 85)

CLUB SIDE: Hibernian (Scotland)

EXPERIENCE: ★ ★ ★ ★

KEY FACT: Very determined, having fought his way back into the team.

NIGERIA

NAME: William Okpara

BORN: 7.5.68

HEIGHT: 6 ft (1 m 83)

CLUB SIDE: Orlando Pirates (South Africa)

EXPERIENCE: ★

KEY FACT: Very commanding in the box.

NAME: Ike Shorunmu

BORN: 16.10.67

HEIGHT: 6 ft 1 (1 m 85)

CLUB SIDE: FC Zurich (Switzerland)

EXPERIENCE: ★

KEY FACT: A fearsome figure with sharp reflexes.

SOUTH AFRICA

NAME: Andre Arendse

BORN: 27.6.67, Cape Town, South Africa

HEIGHT: 6 ft 3 (1 m 91)

CLUB SIDE: Fulham (England)

EXPERIENCE: ★ ★

KEY FACT: His experience could prove vital to the team's chances of success.

AMAZING FACT: Set a record of 693 minutes without conceding a goal in international football.

NAME: Boubaker Zitouni

BORN: 28.1.65, Tunis, Tunisia

HEIGHT: 5 ft 10 (1 m 78)

CLUB SIDE: Club Africain de Tunis (Tunisia)

EXPERIENCE: ★ ★ ★

KEY FACT: His agility is his strongest weapon.

CAMEROON

NAME: Jacques Songo'o

BORN: 17.3.64, Sackbayme, Cameroon

HEIGHT: 6 ft (1 m 83)

CLUB SIDE: Deportivo La Coruña (Spain)

EXPERIENCE: ★ ★ ★ ★ ★

KEY FACT: Another extrovert Cameroon goalkeeper.

AMAZING FACT: Voted the Best Goalkeeper in Spain after the 1996-97 season.

NAME: Vincent Ongandzi

BORN: 22.11.75, Meyos, Cameroon

HEIGHT: 5 ft 11 (1 m 80)

CLUB SIDE: Unisport de Bafang (Cameroon)

EXPERIENCE: ★ ★

WORLD CUP 1998

23 COOL KEEPERS

MOROCCO

NAME: Abdel Kader El Brazi

BORN: 5.11.64, Berkane, Morocco

HEIGHT: 6 ft (1 m 83)

CLUB SIDE: Forces Armées Royales de Rabat (Morocco)

EXPERIENCE: ★ ★ ★ ★ ★

KEY FACT: A reputation for bravery, and also good with crosses.

PARAGUAY

NAME: Jose Luis Chilavert

BORN: 27.7.65, Luque, Paraguay

HEIGHT: 6 ft 2 (1 m 88)

CLUB SIDE: Velez Sarsfield (Argentina)

EXPERIENCE: ★ ★ ★ ★ ★

KEY FACT: His long clearances are an effective form of attack.

AMAZING FACT: Often takes penalties and free kicks.

PARAGUAY

NAME: Ruben Ruiz Diaz
BORN: 11.11.69, Asunción, Paraguay
HEIGHT: 6 ft 2 (1 m 88)
CLUB SIDE: Monterrey (Mexico)
EXPERIENCE: ★ ★
KEY FACT: Lacks Chilavert's flamboyance but is technically a better keeper.

ARGENTINA

NAME: Herman Burgos
BORN: 16.4.69, Buenos Aires, Argentina
HEIGHT: 5 ft 9 (1 m 75)
CLUB SIDE: River Plate (Argentina)
EXPERIENCE: ★ ★ ★ ★ ★
KEY FACT: An experienced goalkeeper who has 'been there, seen it and done it'!

NAME: Carlos Roa
BORN: 15.8.69, Santa Fé, Argentina
HEIGHT: 6 ft 3 (1 m 91)
CLUB SIDE: Mallorca (Spain)
EXPERIENCE: ★ ★
KEY FACT: Strong, athletic and a vital part of the team.

COLOMBIA

NAME: Farid Mondragon
BORN: 21.6.71, Cali, Colombia
HEIGHT: 6 ft 3 (1 m 91)
CLUB SIDE: Independiente (Argentina)
EXPERIENCE: ★ ★
KEY FACT: Solid and reliable.

NAME: Oscar Cordoba
BORN: 3.2.70, Cali, Colombia
HEIGHT: 6 ft 1 (1 m 85)
CLUB SIDE: Boca Juniors (Argentina)
EXPERIENCE: ★ ★★ ★
KEY FACT: Superb shot stopper.
AMAZING FACT: Was once nearly hit by a bomb thrown on to the pitch during a league game in Argentina.

CHILE

NAME: Nelson Tapia
BORN: 22.9.66, Rancagua, Chile
HEIGHT: 5 ft 11 (1 m 80)
CLUB SIDE: Universidad Catolica (Chile)
EXPERIENCE: ★ ★
KEY FACT: Doesn't command his area very well.
AMAZING FACT: Played for the FIFA All Stars against Brazil in 1996.

USA

NAME: Tony Meola

BORN: 21.2.67, New Jersey, USA

HEIGHT: 6 ft 1 (1 m 85)

CLUB SIDE: New Jersey Metrostars (USA)

EXPERIENCE: ★ ★ ★ ★ ★

KEY FACT: Brave and reliable.

AMAZING FACT: The most capped USA keeper ever.

USA

NAME: Kasey Keller
BORN: 29.11.69, Washington, USA
HEIGHT: 6 ft 2 (1 m 88)
CLUB SIDE: Leicester City (England)
EXPERIENCE: ★ ★
KEY FACT: Cool and confident, with very sharp reflexes.

JAMAICA

NAME: Warren Barrett
BORN: 7.9.70, St James, Jamaica
HEIGHT: 6 ft 2 (1 m 88)
CLUB SIDE: Violet Kickers (Jamaica)
EXPERIENCE: ★ ★ ★ ★ ★
KEY FACT: Can be inconsistent but is very good coming off his line.
AMAZING FACT: The most capped Jamaican ever.

NAME: Aaron Lawrence
BORN: 8.11.70, Westmoreland, Jamaica
HEIGHT: 6 ft 2 (1 m 88)
CLUB SIDE: Reno FC (Jamaica)
EXPERIENCE: ★ ★
KEY FACT: A steady understudy to Barrett.

MEXICO

NAME: Jorge Campos
BORN: 25.10.66, Acapulco, Mexico
HEIGHT: 5 ft 10 (1 m 78)
CLUB SIDE: LA Galaxy (USA)
and Cruz Azul (Mexico)
EXPERIENCE: ★ ★ ★ ★ ★
KEY FACT: Very flamboyant but can lose
concentration.
AMAZING FACT: Famous for
introducing Day-Glo coloured keepers'
shirts into the game!

NAME: Adolfo Rios
BORN: 11.12.66, Uruapan, Mexico
HEIGHT: 5 ft 9 (1 m 75)
CLUB SIDE: Necaxa (Mexico)
EXPERIENCE: ★ ★
KEY FACT: A superb all-round keeper.

JAPAN

NAME: Yoshikatsu Kawaguchi
BORN: 15.8.75, Shizuoka, Japan
HEIGHT: 5 ft 11 (1 m 80)
CLUB SIDE: Yokohama Marinos (Japan)
EXPERIENCE: ★ ★
KEY FACT: Outstanding shot-stopper
with excellent reflexes.

NAME: Kenichi Simokawa

BORN: 14.5.70, Gifu, Japan

HEIGHT: 6 ft 2 (1 m 88)

CLUB SIDE: United Ichihara (Japan)

EXPERIENCE: ★

KEY FACT: A natural talent who many believe could make a mark in the tougher European leagues.

W O R L D C U P 1 9 9 8

IRAN

NAME: Ahmed reza Abadzadeh
CLUB SIDE: Pirouzi (Iran)
KEY FACT: Confident and courageous.

SAUDI ARABIA

NAME: Mohammed Daye
BORN: 1972
HEIGHT: 6 ft 2 (1 m 88)
CLUB SIDE: Al Tai (Saudi Arabia)
EXPERIENCE: ★ ★ ★ ★ ★
KEY FACT: Very agile and fast.

SOUTH KOREA

NAME: Kim Byung-ji
BORN: 8.4.70, Pusan, South Korea
HEIGHT: 6 ft 1 (1 m 85)
CLUB SIDE: Ulsan Hyundai (Korea)
EXPERIENCE: ★ ★
KEY FACT: Great handling skills and a superb kicker.